Co-Parenting After Divorce

How to Raise Happy, Healthy Children in Two-Home Families

Diana Shulman, J.D., Ph.D.

Library of Congress

Catalog Card Number: 97-90007

ISBN: 0-9656907-0-9

WinnSpeed Press
14622 Ventura Blvd., Ste. 329
Sherman Oaks, California 91403

Phone   (818) 908 0058
Fax   (818) 909 9209

Cover design by James MacQuarrie

Printed and bound in the
United States of America

Dedication

In loving memory of Jill Shulman
and Flora DiRaffaele.

Acknowledgments

I am indebted to each and every one of my clients who has been willing to share feelings, insights, and opinions about their achievements and setbacks on the road to successful co-parenting. Without them, this book could not have been written.

I am sincerely grateful to my colleagues, Dr. Stephen Rush, Dr. Jody Whitehouse, Dr. Gary Gesler, Jane Waterman, L.C.S.W., Grace White, L.C.S.W., and Shelley E. Hutsler for their help and suggestions.

I also wish to thank Rosaline L. Zukerman, Esq. for her excellent advice concerning the legal aspects of divorce and co-parenting.

To my wonderful friends for their inspiration and encouragement: Robin Baker, Trish Bennett, Lisa Bronson, Joey Levin, Yuko Nomura, Anne O'Connor, Sharon Rakunas, Margaret Rogers, and Carol Wysocki.

To Deborah A. Boggs, Esq., a special thanks for advice on legal matters, editing, and for her encouragement during this entire project.

To Philip for being a constant source of joy and inspiration.

CONTENTS

Introduction

Did you know that ...

✪ your child's experience of your divorce is determined in part by age and maturity level and in part by how you handle the process?

✪ if divorce is mishandled by the adults, children can suffer permanent psychological damage, but if handled well, children from two-home families are as likely to develop into healthy, well-adjusted adults as children from intact families?

Children and adults alike need help recovering from divorce; no one is exempt!

In the midst of my divorce recovery, I looked for an unintimidating and practical guide to help with the adjustment process. I had two requirements in mind:

✪ no war stories about other couples (because no other couples seemed enough like us); and

✪ instant, cut-to-the-chase information (because I was too distraught to read pages and pages of fine print).

When my book search proved unsuccessful, I promised myself that I would someday put my thoughts on the subject of co-parenting in a warm, practical, and easy to read book - one that spoke with the voice of a caring yet sensible friend. The result is *Co-Parenting After Divorce: How to Raise Happy, Healthy Children in Two-Home Families.*

As a psychotherapist and attorney, my belief is that all children need both their mothers and their fathers to participate actively in their development. My hope is that you will remain firmly committed to the principles of co-parenting, especially during those times when the journey is frustrating and difficult.

Diana Shulman, JD, PhD
Los Angeles, California

Chapter One

Basics of Co-Parenting

○ Nobody welcomes divorce; dreams are shattered and lives are turned upside down. And though most of us would welcome news of a decline in the divorce rate, divorce continues to be an unfortunate fact of modern life. "Co-parenting" is a constructive response to the upheaval brought about by divorce.

○ "Co-parenting" simply refers to the co-operative involvement of both mother and father in raising their children after divorce. It is based on the principle that the commitment and devotion of each parent are necessary if children are to emerge from divorce healthy and well-adjusted.

○ If you bristle at the thought of your co-parent's importance and involvement in your children's lives, remember that your children do not share this point of view. They continue to love and need both of you.

⚙ Although certain aspects of two-home parenting are difficult for everyone, co-parenting does not have to be a bad experience for parents or children. Strive to maintain a positive focus; your attitude sets the stage for your children's reactions.

⚙ If you are able to accept your new situation as "different," rather than judging it as "bad" or "harder," you will have an easier time making the transition from a one to two-home family.

⚙ Remember, each of you has something unique to offer to your children. Sometimes this uniqueness becomes apparent only after parents have made the transition from "couple" to "co-parents."

⚙ As a co-parent, you will probably be closer to your children than you were prior to the divorce. In fact, many co-parents find that they spend more quality time with their children after the divorce, particularly if life was stormy before.

⚙ You needn't worry that your children seem to behave somewhat differently around each of you. This is perfectly normal; we all learn to adapt our behavior to fit the company we're keeping and the situations we're in.

✪ As co-parents, you will "model" more flexible, less rigid parenting roles for your children; Dad cooks and sews on a button, Mom learns the art of bicycle repair. In a world that is constantly changing, this type of flexibility can be an asset.

✪ As a result of your divorce and co-parenting arrangement, your children will no longer be observing a dead, non-functional, conflict-ridden, or otherwise dysfunctional marriage. In the years to come, you may find that you develop a better relationship with your "ex" than you had during your marriage.

✪ Children raised in two-home families have the opportunity to develop their problem-solving and people skills by interacting with two separate heads of household and by successfully adapting to differences between the two.

✪ Your children will have a less idealized, more realistic view of relationships. This may help them to make better choices of partners later on in life.

✪ As your co-parenting relationship develops, you will have responsible, caring back-up and relief from the task of of full-time parenting, without having to rely on baby-sitters or nannies.

✪ Finally, there will be extra time available and with it, additional opportunities for you to renew past commitments to personal growth and change.

Personal Notes:

Chapter Two

Creating a Co-Parenting Plan

⚙ Any type of written parenting plan necessarily ends some of the spontaneity that was part of life prior to divorce. Many parents are profoundly saddened by the thought that they will no longer be seeing their children on a casual or everyday basis.

⚙ Even when relations between co-parents are amicable, hammering out the parenting plan is a formidable undertaking. Not only must parents agree on how best to share time with the children, but agreement must also be reached on issues such as child support, health care, religious training, schooling, holidays, vacations, and dispute resolution.

⚙ When relations between co-parents are strained, the task of creating a parenting plan can become overwhelming and is best undertaken with outside help (see, Chapter Three, Choosing an Attorney).

✪ Numerous co-parenting formats are possible. For instance, co-parents could opt to parcel up the week on a percentage basis (80/20, 70/30, or 60/40) or agree to a 1 week on, 1 week off schedule. Four examples follow:

• Parent A: Alternate weekends plus Thursday overnights
• Parent B: Alternate weekends plus Monday, Tuesday, and Wednesday overnights

• Parent A: Weeks 1 and 2 of each month
• Parent B: Weeks 3 and 4 of each month

• Parent A: Sunday morning through Tuesday morning
• Parent B: Tuesday afternoon through Sunday morning

• Parent A: Monday afternoon through Thursday morning
• Parent B: Thursday afternoon through Monday morning

✪ The objective of all such plans is to allow the children sufficient consecutive days in each home to foster a sense of living with, rather than visiting, each parent.

✿ What matters more than the particulars of any plan is the on-going commitment of both parents to cooperate in the raising of their children post-divorce. Specifics will always be decided on a case by case basis.

✿ Careful consideration must be given to the ages of the children and their special needs for closeness with a particular parent.

✿ Sometimes this will mean making different arrangements for each child. For example, a 4 year old girl might have consecutive overnights with each parent while her 18 month old brother would spend all overnights with Mom and specified daytime periods with Dad.

✿ Bearing in mind the uniqueness of each situation, the following are general guidelines, by age group, for determining the amount and sequence of overnights. For more detailed information, see Chapter Nine.

✿ *Newborns and Toddlers.* All overnights should be with the co-parent who was most involved with caretaking prior to separation (Co-Parent A). Day visits by Co-Parent B, gradually becoming outings and slowly increasing in length from 1 hour up to 6 hours, are suggested.

✪ *Pre-Schoolers.* When the child seems ready for overnights, begin with one overnight per week with Co-Parent B. If both co-parents are involved caretakers and overnights are going well, increase to 2 non-consecutive nights per week and then 2 consecutive nights (3 non-consecutive nights involve too much back and forth).

✪ *Primary School.* Children in this age range are usually comfortable with longer parental absences and so are ready for larger blocks of consecutive overnights. Weeks can be divided so that the child spends up to 3 to 4 consecutive days with each co-parent. Alternating full weeks is not recommended for this age group.

✪ *Preteens and Teenagers.* As long as important developmental activities that depend upon groups and institutions outside of the family (friends, school, sports, extra-curricular activities) are allowed to progress, dividing the week equally or alternating weeks can be workable plans for these age groups.

✪ However, if travel between homes is causing too much interruption or discontinuity, attempting to divide parenting time into roughly equal parts may no longer be optimal. Your teens and pre-teens may begin to complain about the difficulties involved in shuttling back and forth.

✿ Parents may find it necessary to designate one home as the primary residence when older children are involved. As a result, your teen or pre-teen may spend less time at the non-primary home (for instance, one mid-week overnight and selected weekends), so as to accommodate activities important to his or her growth and development.

✿ Adhere to your parenting plan so that your children have guilt-free, conflict-free access to both homes as well as a weekly schedule upon which everyone can rely for purposes of making plans and appointments. Don't put your children in the position of having to choose one co-parent over the other.

✿ Plan for the unexpected! Have guidelines for what will happen on days when a child is ill, when school holidays fall on work days, or when one co-parent will be unavailable on his or her days with the children.

✿ In the event that you and your co-parent are unable to reach agreement, child custody issues will be decided by a judge. Note that in some jurisdictions, including California, confidential mediation sessions with a counselor appointed by the court are required before a hearing can take place.

○ When a parenting plan is presented to a court, the parties lose control of the outcome. You may be better off negotiating a less than perfect out-of-court settlement rather than taking a chance on an agreement ordered by the court.

○ No plans are ever final. Because children are involved, all plans are modifiable in the event of changed circumstances.

○ As one of a large and growing number of co-parents, feel free to reject the outmoded term "broken home." Remind yourself that your home is no more "broken" than anyone else's. In fact, your household may function better than many intact family homes.

○ Far more important than a common address is the fact that the parents in your two-home family treat each other and their children with kindness, respect, and attention.

Personal Notes:

Chapter Three

Choosing an Attorney

☼ Prepare to shop around; this is not a decision to be made lightly!

☼ Request a 1 hour, no fee interview with at least 3 attorneys who've come well-recommended before making a selection. Your objective is to find someone who can help you realize your goals while sidestepping protracted, expensive litigation.

☼ Remember, in the hotly contested cases, more often than not, the only real winners are the lawyers.

☼ Ask about years of experience and specialization in family law, experience with co-parenting issues before local judges, percentage of cases settled before trial, and percentage of cases "won" at trial.

✪ Ask about retainers and hourly rates (does he or she bill in 1/4 hour increments only, or are 2 or 5 minute phone calls also billed as 15 minute calls?). Will other attorneys or associates with lower hourly rates be working on your case?

✪ Are you comfortable with this attorney? Is he or she someone around whom you'll feel free to express yourself? Does this person seem to empathize with your problems and understand the issues you feel are important?

✪ Will he or she be easily accessible when you call? Will you receive copies of all documents? Will you be able to get tax and financial advice if you need it?

✪ If you would like to be an active participant in your litigation, ask what you can do on your end to keep costs down. Would it be agreeable if you were to write drafts of letters, prepare background information for affidavits and declarations, summarize financial materials, etc. so as to minimize your expenses?

✪ Ask any potential attorneys for their opinion about the impact of protracted litigation on children.

○ Unless you feel it is in your best interests to hire a flame thrower, ask candidates whether they will work with opposing counsel to get a constructive dialogue going between the two sides (rather than setting up two warring camps).

○ Perhaps you, your "ex," and your two attorneys can sit down early on in the litigation process to hammer out an agreement that satisfies everyone (without having to go through several sets of interrogatories, depositions, motions and court-ordered settlement conferences).

○ Once you've selected an attorney, keep your costs as low as possible by being organized and by preparing for meetings and phone calls in advance. Consolidate your questions into one phone call, and save the hand-holding for friends or family; lawyers are too expensive.

○ Ask to receive itemized bills instead of just summaries of work done and time spent on your case. Keep a record of time spent with your attorney - phone calls, court appearances, conferences - to catch any errors in billing.

○ Do not assume anyone but you will end up footing the bill even if you are asking the Court for an order to have your "ex" pay. You may get less than you expect.

✪ Before you finally decide to go the usual route where each party hires a separate attorney, consider the possibility of engaging the services of a qualified mediator to resolve your differences. Divorce mediation, a process which combines family counseling and legal advice, provides several advantages over the adversarial legal process.

✪ Divorce mediation is cheaper, and it's less divisive since both parents work together from the outset to reach an agreement about their children, their property, and child support/alimony. (Nevertheless, think twice about using a mediator if you feel overpowered by your "ex" or if you have a sense that you need someone to act as your advocate).

✪ Mediation is not a public proceeding like a trial, and it's easier for the parties to return to the mediator and work out modifications - in contrast to the adversary system where you may have to start again from ground zero.

✪ Mediation requires several one to two hour sessions over a period of several weeks (or months, if relations are strained) and culminates in the creation of a non-binding agreement. Both parties then submit this agreement to separate consulting attorneys for review and comment.

○ For purposes of agreement review, each party should engage the services of an experienced attorney who appreciates the value of mediated agreements. If you hire an attorney who is uncomfortable or unfamiliar with the mediation process, you are likely to witness the dissection of your carefully crafted agreement.

○ After review by the consulting attorneys, both parties return to the mediator to record any final changes in the agreement. When signed, the agreement is a legally enforceable contract between the parties. If presented to a judge for approval, it becomes a court-ordered judgment of divorce (in some jurisdictions, the parties must submit the agreement to a judge for a determination of fairness).

○ You can use the services of a mediator at any time during the adversary process or you can agree to use a mediator to resolve specific issues, such as those relating to custody, while continuing to work with your separate attorneys.

○ Both parties should separately interview several mediators before a joint selection is made. Ask candidates about their experience and training. Is this someone with whom you'll be comfortable expressing yourself? Interview any potential mediators as you would an attorney (see, pages 11-12).

✪ Ask yourself if the candidate seems unbiased, wise, empathic and fair. Bear in mind that some of the best mediators have a background in either law or counseling.

Personal Notes:

Chapter Four

Telling Your Children

☼ Once you have made an absolutely final decision to divorce (as opposed to experiments and
trial separations), both parents need to explain
to all the children that they have an important
and serious family matter to discuss.

☼ Your children will be pained by the decision
and this cannot be avoided. Do not "use" their
discomfort as a reason to leave out important
information or avoid the discussion altogether.

☼ You will be saddened upon telling them, and
you needn't be afraid to show your sorrow. It's
natural and appropriate (do not, however, pick
a time to tell them when you are at an all time
low or feeling out of control).

☼ Your children need to see that although Mom
and Dad are sad, things are going to be okay. Remember, your children take their cues from you.

○ Look for a time to tell your children when none of them is particularly upset or worried, otherwise you run the risk that they will somehow misconstrue the information and wind up feeling responsible or at fault.

○ Explain the divorce to your children in an age-appropriate way, bearing in mind that if you fail to provide reasons or sufficient detail about the break-up, they may blame themselves. Never allow a child to shoulder the responsibility for the parents' divorce!

○ Do not have this discussion while going for a drive! You cannot make sustained eye contact in a car, and you certainly cannot devote your full attention to the matter at hand while driving.

○ Plan in advance with your co-parent what you are going to say and how much detail you are going to provide. Use an outline if you're worried that your thinking may be clouded.

○ Don't rush; give your children time to comprehend what you are saying and react to the news.

○ Do not break the news to your children separately; they need each other at this time. Moreover, they may feel excluded by separate discussions and may not trust that they are being presented with the same information.

✪ If your children are of mixed ages, you can provide more "grown up" information to the older children separately once the group meeting has ended.

✪ Bearing in mind that the parents' marriage often becomes the model of marriage in the minds of children, you might say:

"When people get married it's usually forever and we hope when you get married, it will be that way, but sometimes, something goes wrong and then moms and dads feel like they can't live together anymore, and that's what happened with your Mom (Dad) and me."

✪ In response to your children's "why?" questions, you might say:

"We're fighting too much (or we're too mad/sad) when we're together and that isn't good for anybody."

✪ Do not make accusations or discuss the faults of either parent.

✪ To discourage hopes that Mom and Dad will reconcile, you might say:

"We've given this decision a lot of thought, we've looked at it in many different ways and

it is a final decision. Even though it feels very sad, this decision is not going to change."

✿ To reassure your children, you might say:

"We will always be your Mom and Dad, that will never change, and we will always love you and take good care of you, but from now on we will take care of you from two homes instead of one. You will spend time with Daddy at his home and with Mommy at her home. This was a very hard decision to make, and it's going to mean a lot of changes, but it's going to work out fine in the end if we all talk about our feelings and work together."

✿ To elicit open discussion, you might say:

"Things are going to feel very different for a while, so don't be afraid to ask us lots of questions, and tell us what you're feeling or thinking about. We know this is difficult for you and we want to answer all your questions as best we can."

✿ Provide details on the "second home," where it is and what it's like, and the basic mechanics of the parenting plan you've worked out. Be careful to reassure your children that Mom and Dad are divorcing each other and not them.

⚙ It's best for the children if the parents do not separate immediately after the family meeting. Regardless of how much you want "out," you owe your children some time to process this information.

⚙ On the other hand, do not wait too long. Prolonging the actual separation can be confusing; it creates the impression that the divorce isn't really happening and leaves everyone in limbo.

⚙ If there have been no sudden departures and both parents still reside in the original family home, try not to separate until a week or two after the family meeting.

⚙ This will allow your children time to grasp the information, ask questions, air their feelings, and start coming to terms with their new reality.

⚙ You will not be able to answer all of your children's questions, nor will you be able to magically erase their sadness, anger, fear and confusion.

⚙ Some questions call for information that is too "grown up" or too personal. Let your children know that you will be able to give them more information when they are older.

○ At times there will be nothing more you can do but encourage them to talk while you listen well and remind yourself that time is a great healer.

○ Adjusting to divorce will be an on-going process for your children. It isn't something that gets settled "once and for all."

○ As time goes by, teach your children the lessons to be learned from your mistakes.

○ Give them age-appropriate information about the factors that caused your divorce ("We were too young, too different or didn't communicate" or "We should have just remained good friends").

○ Be sure to convey the message that divorce does not happen to everybody and does not have to happen to them!

Personal Notes:

Chapter Five

Do's and Don'ts

Love and Respect

✵ Give your children the space to believe that both of you are good and loving parents. Your children usually do not think of either of you as the "more loving" or "better" parent. Unless you are somehow attempting to persuade them otherwise, they will simply love and respect each of you.

✵ Conveying messages to your children that you are the "better" parent implies that your co-parent is somehow deficient or careless. This will trouble your children and may lead to depression and lowered self-esteem.

✵ Look at your divorce through your children's eyes. As much as you may be glad you've separated or divorced, your children are not. They continue to need and love both Mom and Dad and want both of you to be involved in their lives.

Criticism

⚙ Do not undermine your co-parent's authority in front of your children.

⚙ If you disagree with some aspect of your co-parent's behavior, contain yourself and bring up the issue when the children are not around. If you make the effort, you will find that there is ample opportunity to discuss differences when your children are out of earshot.

⚙ Exceptions must, of course, be made for those situations where your co-parent's actions are sufficiently inappropriate or dangerous to warrant immediate intervention for your children's safety.

⚙ Otherwise, avoid the kind of interventions or criticisms that create rifts and doubts. Everyone has faults, and while some measure of disagreement or criticism is normal, harping on your co-parent's limitations is a poor idea.

⚙ Remind yourself that your child's self-esteem will be adversely affected by a belief that either parent is inadequate.

⚙ Be supportive of your co-parent! Being supportive, however, does not mean sugarcoating situations that are obviously toxic.

○ If your co-parent shows signs of a physical or emotional disorder that negatively impacts his or her caretaking abilities, give your children an age-appropriate explanation ("Mom/Dad has been having a problem with drinking, she/he will be able to see you as soon as she/he is feeling better and when the problem is under control").

○ When your children have a criticism of the other parent, just listen, rather than joining in or agreeing.

○ If you feel the point is legitimate, acknowledge their feelings ("You're right, Mom/Dad has been late a lot this month"), and encourage them to take up the issue with your co-parent, but don't assume that your children want you to attack their Dad or Mom.

○ If your children suspect that you have a negative point of view about your co-parent, they may follow suit in an effort to please you. This harms their capacity to think for themselves and undermines relations with your co-parent– a result that is good for no one.

Competition

○ Many parents report feeling competitive with their co-parent from time to time regarding their children's love and attention.

○ While this is understandable, do your best not to telegraph the message or act on these feelings!

○ Competitiveness suggests winners and losers, and striving to win may blind you to your children's best interests. For instance, in your efforts to be the "nicest" parent, you may fail to be a good disciplinarian.

○ Relax and remember that your children love each of you.

○ If your children make unfavorable comparisons between the two of you, remind them that you are two separate people, each trying to do the best you can for them, and that you each have your own set of strengths and weaknesses.

○ Teach your children to accept differences.

Fighting

○ If you and your "ex" must do battle, shield your children from the intense encounters. A child's sense of security and self-esteem can be damaged by repeated exposure to combative parents.

○ If your "ex" attempts to fight with you in front of the children, do not participate. The less you participate, the less your "ex" will continue to argue.

❁ In those situations when your "ex" is too bitter or angry to exercise restraint, you must continue to respond calmly so as to defuse the situation.

❁ You needn't worry about sheltering your children from all adult conflict. If there's going to be a good, clean argument with fair and respectful disagreement, children can benefit from seeing and hearing it.

❁ Disagreement and anger are an inevitable part of life. Your children will learn to see conflict - with anger constructively expressed - as one form of healthy interaction between adults.

Relaying Messages

❁ Do not use your children as messengers ("Tell your Dad to start cleaning your clothes!"). Questions which contain subtle judgments or criticisms can lead your children to feel that their parents are failing to take good care of them ("Did your Mom wash your hair today?").

❁ Do not use your children for espionage ("Who was that man who answered the phone?" or "Did your Dad move offices?"). Using your children for your own adult purposes forces them to take sides and makes them feel conflicted and disloyal.

✪ Do not use your children to negotiate adult issues ("Remember to ask your Mom/Dad if you can leave school early; if I suggest it, she'll/he'll say no.").

✪ Even the most innocuous kind of probing and questioning can worry children by placing them in the midst of parental issues. If you have a question for your co-parent, ask it yourself! Never turn your children into friends or treat them as "pseudo" adults by burdening them with grown-up concerns. Leave adult issues for the adults.

Personal Notes:

Chapter Six

Adjusting to Differences

✪ Even the most co-operative of co-parents can expect to have differences of opinion about various aspects of child-raising from time to time. Good, stable marriages are no different; you find that certain issues cannot be resolved regardless of how well two people communicate.

✪ Listed below are everyday areas where co-parents may clash:

(a) rules, discipline (homework, chores, bedtime, manners, sit-down meals, neatness, cleanliness)

(b) recreation (amount and/or type of activities, movies or TV programs)

(c) money (spending habits, toys and gifts, disputes over "who pays")

(d) health (alternative medicine, nutrition, junk food, fast food)

(e) religious training and upbringing

✪ There is no rule that you have to like everything your co-parent does. Moreover, you can comment on your co-parent's "limitations" and differences provided that you do so without sounding overly critical or harsh.

✪ For instance, "I know your Mom feels it's healthier to be a vegetarian, and when you're at Mom's you can eat the way she does. I have vegetables plus meat in my diet, and when you're here, I'll cook them for you." Or, "I know your Dad wants you to visit Grandma on Saturday, and when you're with him, he'll take you. When you're here, we can still do our Saturday morning nature hikes."

✪ When issues involve personal preference or opinion only, do not say to your children, "Mom/Dad is wrong about that." Encourage them to see things more objectively by saying instead, "Your Mom/Dad and I have different opinions about that."

✪ It's important for children to understand differences between people without feeling they must decide who is "right" or which way is "better."

○ If, during the marriage, you and your co-parent divided the task of disciplining the children (typically, one of the parents is the "heavy"), you may need to become more of a disciplinarian now that you are a co-parent.

○ Learn to set reasonable, age-appropriate rules and limits. Explain your expectations and the consequences of failing to meet them.

○ Reward good behavior with compliments, smiles, hugs or praise. Be consistent and make it clear that it is bad behavior, as opposed to a "bad child," that gets punished.

○ If you can do so without compromising your own parenting style, work with your co-parent to establish some joint rules to help heal the rupture caused by the divorce (for example, no television/video games until homework is done or a jointly enforced 11:30 P.M. weekend curfew for teenagers).

○ Be sure your children understand both the rules and the consequences of breaking them.

○ Do not expect your co-parent to enforce rules or exact penalties for rules that he/she doesn't necessarily believe in and which are rules in your home only.

✪ Infractions of rules that are rules in your home only must be handled during your time with the children.

✪ Never send a child to the other parent's home because of "bad" behavior!

✪ Differences between co-parents can work to everyone's advantage. Take responsibility for those areas of parenting where you have a particular aptitude or interest and encourage your co-parent to do the same.

✪ For instance, if you like structure, be the parent who prepares the monthly calendar showing Mom's/Dad's days, school events, vacation days, doctor's appointments, Little League games, gymnastic recitals, and make a copy for both homes.

✪ Stress your co-parent's talents and strengths to your children ("Your Dad is good at math, why don't you ask him for help with your algebra?").

✪ Encourage your children to appreciate the uniqueness of both Mom and Dad, and everyone will benefit.

✪ When you are troubled by differences in parenting styles, ask yourself if the issue at hand is really worth going to the mat about.

✪ If it is, then you must take up the issue with your co-parent for the sake of your children. However, if your child sits at the dinner table at your home but has dinner in front of the television at your co-parent's, this is probably not worth worrying about.

✪ If Mom does one thing and Dad does another, your children can learn to think independently and one day decide for themselves what they prefer. Show your children that you can tolerate another opinion without being permissive or abandoning your own position.

✪ Don't worry so much that you and your co-parent have different styles and different personalities. Your children will not be bewildered by all of the variations.

✪ As long as you are not concerned about negligence or mistreatment, your co-parent has the right to raise his/her children as he or she chooses. For the most part, you are just going to have to live with this, notwithstanding your level of irritation or frustration.

✪ Keep in mind, however, that seemingly minor "style" or disciplinary differences between the parents can sometimes develop into larger problems.

✪ For instance, if your co-parent habitually relaxes agreed upon rules about bedtime, chores, or homework, your children may begin to form inaccurate and unrealistic perceptions about responsibilities and limits ("I know it's a school night, Dad, but Mom always lets me watch this show. I'll study my spelling words at breakfast").

✪ While your co-parent may tell you that this type of indulgence is not worth worrying about, the overall effect may be negative. If you and your co-parent have gone to the trouble of establishing some joint rules, make an effort to follow them!

✪ Having one parent be the "good times" parent and the other the "disciplinarian," makes transitions between homes more difficult, damages the co-parenting relationship, and causes children to be confused or unrealistic about what is expected of them.

✪ Adhering to rules and limits is essential if you want to give your children a sense of order, security, and responsibility.

✪ Children will always find it easy, later in life, to adjust to less structure. On the other hand, adjusting to more structure as one gets older, is not easy.

✪ If your co-parent continues to indulge the children, despite your efforts to persuade him/her to do otherwise, enjoy the fact that your kids are going to have good times with the "good times" parent.

✪ Don't ever make your children choose sides or feel guilty for having fun; this is an issue for resolution by the parents.

✪ If the "good times" behavior persists, you can still reinforce the value of routines, rules, and limits without knocking your co-parent ("Looks like all that studying paid off. What a great report card!"). And, whatever you do, don't overdo it! Kids neither like nor benefit from a steady diet of preaching and lecturing.

Bedtime/Curfew

✪ When your children are young, it's important that daily routines are coordinated from home to home so that your kids continue to feel good physically and function well. It also will give them a sense of having a less fragmented life.

✪ For little ones, have two sets of the bedtime "necessities," one for each home: stuffed animals and toys, blankets and bedding, and favorite bedtime stories.

⚙ Try to follow a similar routine at each home, *e.g.*, each parent bathes the child at 8 p.m., begins a bedtime story at about 8:30 p.m., and turns the lights out at 9 p.m. Although it's typical for the co-parent with less time with the children to be indulgent and stretch the rules (particularly bedtime), consistency makes bedtime easier on everyone.

⚙ With this in mind, do not allow your children to "zonk out" on the couch or sleep in your bed, particularly if your co-parent is working hard on having them sleep in their own beds!

⚙ Whether you allow your children to sleep in your bed to relieve your own loneliness or ease your guilt about the divorce, it only interferes with their ability to fall asleep by themselves and undermines their sense of independence.

⚙ The sensuality of sleeping in such close proximity can also stir up sexual feelings – an unintended result that can be confusing and/or frightening.

⚙ If your children are having trouble sleeping alone, offer to stay in their room for 15 or 20 minutes until they relax and fall asleep.

○ When your children are school age, an early bedtime is often dictated by the fact that they must wake up early enough to be ready for school. Any lingering differences between the two homes concerning "lights out" usually get synchronized at this point.

○ Try to work co-operatively for the sake of your children. Do not allow your kids to avoid curfew or other rules by going to the other parent's house. All children, teenagers included, need consistent, clear, and reasonable limits.

Birthdays and Joint Functions

○ For the first several years after divorce, birthdays and other joint celebrations can be a source of stress rather than happiness.

○ It may still be difficult for you to be in the company of your "ex," even just for a few hours.

○ Be mature and remember whose day this is. Choose a format that will allow you to give your child a real celebration (rather than a tense get-together with Dad or Mom just going through the motions).

○ With this in mind, ask yourself how well you and your co-parent are getting along.

✪ Whether you have a jointly planned party, a party thrown by one co-parent to which the other is invited, or separate parties will depend upon the level of co-operation that exists between the two of you.

✪ If you have separate parties now, you can always look forward to the day, a few years down the road, when your relationship has improved sufficiently to allow for a joint celebration.

✪ If it's your first joint celebration and you prefer not to celebrate in either home, ask your child about his/her favorite public setting - a junior gym or amusement area, a park, a restaurant, or other location.

✪ If things have been tense recently, have it clearly understood by all participants that a truce will be in effect for the party: no fighting, no rudeness, no hostility or negativity - instead, only constructive behavior designed to enhance your child's experience of the party.

✪ Check with your child to be sure he/she even wants a party - maybe your older child wants something smaller and quieter. Be flexible and respect your children's wishes; it's their day.

✪ At school functions or other joint events, you must also call a halt to any on-going hostility so that your children will enjoy these occasions. Children benefit by seeing their parents being civil and pleasant to each other. Your behavior will let your children know they can relax and have fun.

✪ With this in mind, save a seat for your "ex" at the school play. Sit near each other at graduations so that the graduate doesn't have to spend his/her time tracking down two different sets of friends and relatives.

✪ Whatever the function, be it a piano recital or a wedding, be mature and keep the spotlight off yourself. Enjoy the occasion! This will help it to become a pleasant memory for everyone involved.

Dating/Remarriage/Stepparents

✪ When you begin dating, do not introduce your children to all your date(s).

✪ Avoid having your dates sleep over when your children are with you. Children are oriented to their own needs and may develop attachments. If relationships are temporary and end, your children may have more disappointments or separations to endure.

○ On the other hand, if you've found someone with whom you are entering a long-term relationship or remarriage, then, of course, it makes sense to think about presenting this new person to your children.

○ Be mindful of the way in which you introduce a new partner to your children. New partners can aggravate tensions by increasing feelings of competition or by pressuring you to spend more time with them and less time with your children.

○ Let your children know how important they are to you so that they do not feel left out or competitive with new partners. Let your new partner know how important it is to you that you and your co-parent have a strong, co-operative relationship. This way he or she will at least know the ground rules.

○ If the initial encounters are handled well, you could save yourself a whole host of future problems.

○ If you are planning to remarry, be sure to prepare your co-parent. Remarriage can stir up a host of insecurities, not the least of which are your co-parent's concerns about being replaced, in his/her children's eyes, by the second husband or wife.

✪ Don't increase the potential for hostility and tension by shocking your co-parent with the news, and don't let your co-parent be the last to hear about your plans.

✪ Many co-parents are surprised by the intensity of their reactions to news of their former partner's remarriage. Expect some repercussions, and remind yourselves to keep your children's best interests at heart.

✪ Remarriage can have a positive effect on your co-parenting relationship by introducing a new person with a more moderate or objective viewpoint into the family.

✪ Long-standing issues or disagreements between co-parents may be resolved more easily due to the influence of the new partner on the remarried co-parent.

✪ In situations where the co-parenting plan is working smoothly, consider having co-parents and new partners meet from time to time.

✪ On the theory that several heads are better than two, a group of co-parents and parents who meet from time to time to discuss issues about the children can be a real help in working through difficult parenting issues.

○ Remarriage is often painful for children. If your children are having trouble accepting your new partner, encourage them to talk this over with you.

○ Encourage your new partner to work on developing his or her own connection with the children (this will take a while if there is to be a genuine bond; don't try to force it on either the stepparent or your child).

○ Often, children feel overwhelmed and fear losing the remarrying parent (or, they may worry about losing their "real" Mom or Dad because there is a new stepparent). Reassure them that no one is going to be lost or go away.

○ Adjusting to remarriage, step-brothers and sisters is a complicated matter that takes time. Consider a support group or family therapy if problems persist.

○ If the situation is reversed (the children are fine, but it's you who does not feel kindly towards your co-parent's new partner), remind yourself that your feelings are not the only ones that count.

○ Your children may have many good reasons to be fond of their Mom's or Dad's new mate.

✪ Do not make your children feel guilty about liking their stepparents, instead encourage respect ("I know she isn't your mother, but she's your Dad's wife, and she's in charge in her house").

✪ Keep an open mind; you may ultimately consider it an advantage to have this person in your two home family.

Grandparents and Relatives

✪ Even if you're glad you're no longer part of your "ex's" family, don't assume your children are. They will want to continue relationships with loving grandparents and relatives on your ex's side and will experience unnecessary losses if these relationships are suddenly cut off.

✪ Maintaining contact with grandparents and other relatives helps your children learn that all relationships are not temporary.

✪ Loving relatives are "anchors" in the world and will enrich your children's sense of family. Connections with extended family are also reassuring; one can never be loved by too many people!

✪ Grandparents, in particular, can have a steady-
ing, positive effect on a child. Loving grandparents can make important contributions to your
children's self-esteem and help them grow to be
mature, well-adjusted adults.

✪ Let the grandparents on your co-parent's side
know that you want your children to have a
strong relationship with them. Call or write
them to dispel any notions they may have to the
contrary.

✪ Relax and be flexible about trading days (or
giving extra time) when your co-parent's out-of-
town relatives are available on one of your days.
These are special treats for your children; be
generous with the time.

Hoarding Clothes and Toys

✪ Often when parents buy particular toys or
clothing (or receive them as gifts from their
friends or relatives), they become possessive
and unwilling to allow these items to travel to
the other home.

✪ Or, one parent may especially like an article of
clothing that the other parent has bought for
the child, and see to it that the child never
wears it on days when he/she is going back to
the other parent's house.

○ With the exception of large items that do not travel easily or well, hoarding clothing or toys reflects the parent's concern with his or her own selfish interests rather than the best interests of the child.

○ Petty though it may be, this issue can be a source of continual parental squabbling, particularly during the times when children are being picked up or dropped off at either home.

○ If you find yourself guilty of hoarding on occasion, remind yourself that the items question are your child's property; graciously send these items off to the other home, knowing your child will get even more enjoyment and use out of them.

○ If the other parent's hoarding of clothing or toys is an issue, make a request of your co-parent (not your child) that certain items be returned.

○ Point out the negative consequences for your child (for instance, your co-parent has managed to accumulate most of the warm clothing at the other home).

○ If your co-parent ignores your request and continues to stockpile certain items, quit overpacking. If you can afford to, buy duplicates of the item in question and let this issue go!

✪ When you are most annoyed by your co-parent's hoarding, remind yourself that this behavior is time-limited. As your children get older, they will naturally see to it that this problem gets corrected.

✪ If parental forgetting of clothes or toys is the issue, help your children take on more and more responsibility for remembering to bring their own things. Even little ones can make choices about which clothes and toys to pack if you give them some guidance.

✪ When your children forget to pack or collect their favorite items, remind them that it is up to them, not Mom or Dad, to remember. This will help your children develop into responsible young adults.

Holidays

✪ Most co-parents celebrate significant holidays with their children in alternate years. This is not a reason to give in to melancholy or depression or to abandon the traditions and holidays you used to observe before the divorce.

✪ Holiday traditions and celebrations create a sense of permanence and stability for you and your children. Though painful memories may emerge during the first few years, rituals can be comforting and may eventually give everyone an opportunity to heal divorce-related wounds.

✿ Make your home feel like a real family home by continuing to celebrate holidays that are special to you. Failing to celebrate the holidays means depriving your children of family memories, the fun of making decorations, and enjoying other holiday rituals. There's every reason to keep on celebrating.

✿ Pay attention to how your children are reacting to their first holiday season without both Mom and Dad present.

✿ Encourage discussion about the fact that things might seem sad or unfamiliar so that your children will feel free to air their upset or discomfort.

✿ Don't insist that everything be "fine." If your children miss the other parent, encourage them to make a phone call. Everyone will feel better.

✿ Enjoy your new two-home family. Celebrate the "old" holidays, and make it a point to celebrate some new ones: half birthdays, pet birthdays, annual home video interview night, family costume parties.

✿ Invite your friends and your children's friends over to your home as you would have before. Carry on with your life!

✪ If your children aren't with you on a particular holiday, make plans with friends or family. If you just don't feel like celebrating in any sort of elaborate way, then don't! Simplifying your life is sometimes just what the doctor ordered. Enjoy the time off and save the elaborate celebrations for alternate years when you are with your children.

✪ On the other hand, if you find it especially important to celebrate a particular holiday with your children every year, you can always celebrate the weekend before or the weekend after in years when your children are with your co-parent. Most kids will be able to handle two celebrations of their favorite holidays!

✪ Whatever you do, plan well, plan in advance, and stick to your plans.

✪ As your children get older, consult with them about their preferences, remembering that even though their preferences and opinions may be strong, they still need you to make the rules and set the limits. The parents, not the children, are in charge!

Money: Expenses/Lifestyle/Gifts

✪ Not surprisingly, one of the major reasons for continuing hostility between co-parents is money.

⊕ The question, "Are you paying (or am I paying)?" comes up over and over in a variety of settings (clothing, extra-curricular activities, music lessons, contact lenses, braces, private school, camp, college, weddings).

⊕ Part of the problem lies in the stereotypical fears of each co-parent: men are overly concerned about being exploited to the point of bankruptcy and women are preoccupied with powerlessness and poverty.

⊕ Ask yourself if these are realistic worries in the context of your co-parenting situation. If they aren't, stop acting as if they were!

⊕ Whatever you do, keep your children out of your money struggles! Children are ill-equipped to handle these issues and can become overwhelmed with worries about their ability to "make it." Unfortunately, these worries may follow them into adulthood.

⊕ Disagreements over money may involve:

(a) violation of child support agreements, or changed economic circumstances of either parent.

(b) one parent paying for something which he/she considers to be the other parent's responsibility, either in whole or in part.

(c) one parent living in the original family home while the other lives in a small apartment.

(d) one parent enjoying significant buying power while the other lives on a strict budget.

(e) one parent buying lavish gifts for the children while the other can afford just the bare necessities.

✪ As a result of divorce, there is often some disparity in co-parent purchasing power. If so, you are going to have to come to terms with this reality and advise your children accordingly.

✪ Unfortunately, it is true that on average women do suffer more harm than men as a result of divorce, but if you don't earn as much as your co-parent, don't waste your energy on bitterness. Nobody owes you a living.

✪ If you are the co-parent who is living in a small apartment, explain to your kids that small homes contain just as much love as big homes and that everyone can enjoy themselves just as well in humbler surroundings.

✪ If you are the co-parent with reduced buying power, explain to your children that simple or homemade gifts can be even more special than expensive ones.

❂ Remember that finance is not an area for children. Do not burden your children with the details of your money troubles or bring up financially related complaints about the other parent.

❂ Children need to have only enough information to allow them to form realistic expectations about their lifestyle (*e.g.*, "We can only go out to eat once in a while, it's too expensive right now for our budget").

❂ Anxieties about finance require adult attention. If you need help straightening out your financial future or simply want to let your hair down, call a friend or seek out professional advice.

Phone Calls

❂ Speak with your children by telephone on days when they are with your co-parent. Phone contact allows your children to integrate both aspects of their lives and will accelerate their divorce recovery.

❂ As soon as they are old enough, teach your children both phone numbers. Write down your co-parent's number in a conspicuous place (or store it in the memory of your automatic dial feature) and clearly mark it "Mom" or "Dad." Let your children know that both parents are just a phone call away.

✪ If your co-parent has left an answering machine message for your children, let them know this and/or play the message for them. Encourage your children to be respectful and call back.

✪ Young children have limited attention spans so don't expect to have lengthy, detailed conversations, especially if you are seeing each other on a regular basis.

✪ If you hear an unceremonious, "Can I go now?," after getting one syllable answers to your most caring questions, don't worry. This is not a reflection of a lack of love or a sign that you have been forgotten. More than likely, it has to do with the fact that your child is engrossed in some other activity and isn't able to shift gears easily. Be content with a brief exchange rather than forcing your child to stay on the phone. You will have longer, more satisfying conversations as the years go by.

✪ Give your child time and space when he/she is on the phone with your co-parent. Leave the room, and let your child enjoy his/her Mom or Dad.

✪ Don't pick up on the other end and interrupt when you think enough time has elapsed or when you'd like to discuss some adult issues.

✪ Make your own calls to discuss co-parenting issues when your children are out of earshot.

○ Do not make phone calls to your child at times when they're likely to be disruptive - for instance, during the morning school rush, late at night, when you know it's time for meals, homework, bed or bath. Even though you are calling your child, you are still calling a household that is separate and apart from yours. Be considerate.

Schools

○ Many co-parents describe a feeling of dread when the subject of choosing or changing schools comes up, and it's easy to see why.

○ Next to "who has the kids on what days," resolution of the school issue is the single most important determinant of when, where, and how your children will be spending the lion's share of their days.

○ If you tend to lock horns with your co-parent on other issues, there's no reason to suppose that the school issue will be an exception.

○ Anticipate discussion of the following school-related issues: public vs. private, large vs. small, near vs. far (in relation to either parent's home), expensive vs. less expensive, parochial vs. non-sectarian, academically vs. artistically-oriented etc.

○ Whatever else you do, visit all the possible choices. This will help you be objective, rather than falling into the trap of rejecting a wonderful school simply because you suspect it suits some hidden agenda of your co-parent that you do not value.

○ Find out from parents whose children are in the school what its strong points are - some private schools are known for being nurturing, some large public schools for their particular focus on self-esteem.

○ Talk to principals and teachers, remembering that staff has a major effect on the school's "culture" and climate. You may be surprised at the big difference between two open-enrollment, public elementary schools located within minutes of each other.

○ Ask yourselves whether the school will be suitable given your child's particular interests and aptitudes. Would changing schools be too difficult this semester considering all the other changes and adjustments he or she has recently made?

○ How close is each school to the home where your child spends the majority of his or her time?

○ Which schools do his/her friends attend?

○ Is one parent more academically inclined or more able to provide academic supervision?

○ Does one parent's schedule allow him/her to be more available after school and in the evenings to supervise homework?

○ Check to see that the administration and staff of each school are sensitive to issues concerning children from two home families.

○ Make it a point to inform your child's teacher and principal about your family's new status and update them about anything new you've noticed about your child's behavior.

○ Ask that the child's teacher be on the look-out for divorce-related school performance issues (disruptive or aggressive behavior, sadness, apathy, loss of concentration).

○ Request that both parents get copies of all school announcements, report cards, notices and newsletters. If need be, ask the school to change its various administrative forms so there is space for two parents' names and addresses.

✪ Attend "Back to School" nights and parent-teacher conferences. One of the most valuable things you can do for your children is to show that you're interested in their academic life.

✪ Finally, which ever school you select, be sure to keep yourselves focused on the real issue, "How well will the schools we select prepare our children for the demands and challenges that lie ahead?"

Sports and Extra-Curricular Activities

✪ Apart from the obvious benefits to your child, organized team sports and similar extra-curricular activities are a wonderful opportunity for hostile co-parents to see each other on a regular basis in a structured environment on neutral territory.

✪ You will both be rooting for the same team, cheering the same player, and co-operating to make practices and games go smoothly for your child. It's good practice for letting "bygones be bygones."

✪ Unfortunately, sports and extra-curricular activities also provide a fertile ground for continuing disagreement simply because practices, lessons, and competitions can fall on either parent's days with the children.

⚙ If parents are not co-operating closely or one schedules conflicting activities with the child on practice or game days, the child is effectively prevented from participating in the sport or activity, regardless of the child's or other parent's wishes.

⚙ If your child is ready to play a sport or other extra-curricular activity, do not allow your continuing parental struggles to deprive him/her of the wonderful opportunity to learn about teamwork, cooperation, dedication, or the thrill of mastering something new.

⚙ If enrollment in a league sport is stalled because co-parents live in different neighborhoods and cannot agree on a particular league, common sense dictates picking the league closest to the "primary" residence or school, all other things being equal, so as to reduce the child's commuting time.

⚙ As for disagreements over which sport or activity to choose, ask your child about his/her preferences (keeping in mind age, strengths, skills, stamina, and natural abilities). Get organized early. Find out when and where sign-ups are. Talk to your co-parent about starting dates. If he/she is foot dragging, take it upon yourself to sign up your child before you miss a registration deadline.

Social Development: Friends/Playdates

☺ When there is parental disagreement in this area, it is usually because one parent encourages the children to be socially active and to spend time with friends, while the other tends to limit the children's contact with others and strives to occupy the role of "children's closest companion."

☺ A parent cannot be everything to his/her children. By kindergarten, it is vitally important to your child's social development that he/she plays with peers inside and outside of the school environment.

☺ Arrange play dates and social gatherings for your young children. If a school friend's birthday party falls on your weekend, buy a gift and arrange for your child to attend.

☺ See to it that your older children know that their friends are welcome in your home.

☺ Do not use your children to cure your own loneliness or to fill the void in your adult world caused by the divorce. Carve out time for old hobbies and activities, cultivate new interests and friendships, and plan in advance for the days when your children are with your co-parent.

Personal Notes:

Personal Notes:

Chapter Seven

Pick-Ups and Drop-Offs

⊕ Meeting your "ex" to pick up or drop off your children can be an ordeal in the early stages after separation.

⊕ Either or both parents as well as the children may be nervous, sad, or hostile. It may take a while to "calm down" (even after transitions that seem to go smoothly).

⊕ Although you may be far from calm on these occasions, act "as if" you were.

⊕ Pretending that you have the situation well in hand is preferable to losing control or lashing out in front of your children.

⊕ Contain any anxiety or anger you may be feeling, you will have ample opportunity to address problems with your co-parent when your children are not on the scene. Wait!

✪ While frustrating, none of the following is an emergency:

  (a) Your co-parent failed to bring suitable clothing.

  (b) Your co-parent arrived late.

  (c) Your co-parent "honked" to announce his/her arrival with the children and failed to greet you.

  (d) The children looked dirty.

  (e) Your co-parent took the children out for ice cream although you stated earlier that you were preparing dinner.

✪ If tension is high and tempers are flaring, arrange to have pick-ups and drop-offs at day care or school so as to avoid contact with the other parent until things get more peaceful.

✪ If your children feel torn or saddened during transitions involving both parents, make similar arrangements to avoid the discomfort associated with "leaving" one parent for the other.

✪ If no school or day care organization is involved, arrange to have pick-ups and drop-offs at a neutral place – a restaurant, park, or other public site – to minimize the likelihood of conflict or sadness.

⚙ Regardless of where you meet and even if your relationship is amiable, prepare your children for their transitions between homes.

⚙ Let your children know in advance which days are Dad's and which are Mom's by creating a user-friendly calendar that illustrates the division of time.

⚙ On transition days, follow a routine that's predictable and comfortable. Remind them that Mom/Dad will be arriving after lunch, etc. (younger children will need more concrete and frequent reminders).

⚙ To ease the transition, refer to things you know the children will be doing at the other parent's house (*e.g.*, "Daddy's taking you to the beach tomorrow. That's going to be so much fun!").

⚙ Greet your co-parent regardless of his/her demeanor. Always be aware of your "hellos" and "good-byes," even if your co-parent fails to greet you. A warm "Hi, Daddy!" (or "Hi, Mommy!") uttered by you to your co-parent can reduce the tension produced by silence or outright hostility.

⚙ Be mindful of all that you say. Your children are listening and watching even if they appear not to be. No fighting and no discussion of adult issues!

✪ If your co-parent broaches an adult topic, simply say, "Let's talk about it later," in a calm and pleasant voice. Be prepared to sound like a broken record as you may be required to repeat this phrase several times.

✪ Make allowances for readjustment when your children return from your co-parent's home. Keep in mind that every child is unique and will have his or her own particular style of reacting. You might see some crankiness, highs and lows, or a certain amount of restlessness, defiance, or unhappiness.

✪ Remember, there can be a degree of homesickness or culture shock involved in making a transition between two households, particularly if the two parents have widely disparate living situations or parenting styles. Be sensitive.

✪ Figure out something you can do to make transitions less jarring (have a pre-arranged play-date, see a movie, enjoy a walk in the park or a quiet meal in a restaurant, or simply allow your child some alone time at home to readjust). Whatever works, do it!

✪ Help your children air their feelings. When appropriate, ask open-ended questions that help facilitate discussion.

✪ Be able to hear questions and answers from an upset or unhappy child; don't insist that everything be okay.

✪ If your child is teary, find out why. Maybe insufficient time is being spent with the "missed" parent. Maybe the transition is better made at school so the child feels less torn. Whatever you do, acknowledge problems and difficulties.

✪ Give honest, age-appropriate responses. Don't think that by distracting your child or dodging the issues you are helping.

✪ If your children return to your home with complaints about your co-parent, listen empathically without joining in or taking sides (even if you agree), and encourage them to redirect the complaints to the proper party - your co-parent!

✪ Don't jump in, take over, and relay complaints to your co-parent for your children. Instead, teach responsibility and self-sufficiency by encouraging direct conversations with your co-parent. Involve yourself only when you feel the matter is something they are ill-equipped or too young to handle on their own.

✪ If you've had a pick up or drop off where fighting was involved, remind your children that adults have a hard time adjusting to divorce too, and that they may still be showing their anger or sadness through arguing and hot-headed behavior.

✪ If you're the one who's lost control, apologize to your children, and explain what happened ("I'm still mad/sad, having a hard time with our divorce").

✪ Never complain about your co-parent to your children after you've driven off. Instead, reassure your children that they have two loving parents who are doing their best during a difficult time.

✪ Let go of pictures of an ideal marriage as well as pictures of an ideal co-parenting relationship; you and your "ex" may never interact like an ideal couple; if you did, you probably never would have divorced in the first place.

✪ This is not a perfect world, life happens; some forgetfulness, some lateness, some changes in schedules, and other unforeseen problems are bound to occur. Adopt an "I can handle it" attitude.

Personal Notes:

Personal Notes:

Chapter Eight

Transition Anxiety

⚙ Shuttling back and forth between two homes takes some getting used to and may present problems on occasion.

⚙ Do not allow your child to stay with you simply because of complaints about going to the other parent's house. Often this is simply a matter of transition anxiety or an attempt by the child to please you by choosing you. Resist the temptation to "use" these reactions to increase your time with the child.

⚙ On the other hand, forcing an hysterical toddler to make a transition simply because "The Plan" tells you to, is not a good idea either. Use common sense, you may have to momentarily make exceptions to your parenting plan to allow for critical moments in your child's experience.

✪ If your child comes to you and says, "I wanted to stay at Mommy's(Daddy's), I don't want to be here," acknowledge these feelings and empathize with the difficulty in making switches between homes.

✪ Advise your child that at other times he or she might be asking to stay with the other parent (be prepared to be understanding when this happens, even though it may wound you a bit).

✪ Be sure to explain to your children that it is fine with you when they go to the other parent's home, that you want them to have a good relationship with both Mom and Dad, and that it is important for them to spend time with both of you.

✪ Work to overcome transition anxiety by enlisting the help of your co-parent. Readjust the parenting schedule only when experiences of transition anxiety are persistent or repetitive and you feel the child is being harmed by the status quo. Perhaps more time with one of the parents is necessary.

✪ Never use transition anxiety as an opportunity to convince your child that he/she is unhappy with the parenting plan (says Parent, "You're crying because you're not seeing me enough, aren't you?").

⚙ By emphasizing your agenda, you run the risk of confusing your child and damaging relations with your co-parent.

⚙ Do not make transitions between homes more tense by asking your children to keep secrets from the other parent ("Please remember not to tell Mom/Dad we went to the movies on a school night, O.K.?"). Secrets create enormous pressure, encourage dishonesty, and lead to stressful loyalty conflicts. Leave adult issues for the adults!

⚙ Do not make transitions between homes more difficult by displaying your own sadness or becoming melodramatic: (Dad/Mom says tearfully, "Just give me just one more hug, little one, I'm going to miss you so very, very much"). If you are saddened by your children's departure, make every effort to avoid displaying this sadness. If you show that you are okay, your children are apt to feel okay too!

⚙ From time to time, you may suspect that something in particular is behind a sudden reluctance to go to your co-parent's home. If this is the case, ask your child about any unwillingness to go, while reassuring him or her that it's okay to have difficulty adjusting. Encourage a discussion between your child and co-parent on the subject.

○ If there is no special reason of which you're aware, but your child continues to be reluctant to go to the other parent's home, there may be some other factor that's been overlooked.

○ Be prepared to work with your co-parent to help your child resolve this issue. If you don't seem to be getting anywhere, go for family counseling. Don't allow your children to be victimized by your divorce.

Personal Notes:

Chapter Nine

Helping Your Children

☼ Because every child is unique, attempts to classify or predict behavior on the basis of age can be only approximately correct.

☼ Generalizations about children's reactions to their parents' divorce also lack precision and should also be viewed as approximations.

☼ To remedy this problem, please read this chapter in its entirety - from the section on newborns through the section on teenagers.

☼ Reactions of same-aged children to divorce can vary; as a result, you may find something contained in a description of a child older or younger than yours to be more accurate or helpful.

✪ Certain reactions cut across age lines:

  (a) sadness (lack of enthusiasm, withdrawal)

  (b) anger (irritability, low frustration tolerance)

  (c) guilt (feelings of being at fault)

  (d) fear (abandonment or survival issues)

  (e) denial (*e.g.*, belief that Mom and Dad will reunite)

  (f) mistrust (about permanence of relation- ships)

  (g) shame or embarrassment

  (h) regressive behavior (returning to earlier levels of functioning)

✪ Adjusting to the trauma of divorce is difficult for children of all ages. Expect to see some emotional and behavioral difficulties; these are normal under the circumstances.

✪ Encourage your children to express their feel- ings, whatever they may be.

○ If your children look troubled, ask them about it and offer suggestions ("Maybe you miss Mommy and would like to give her a call"). Allowing your children to bottle up their feelings is harmful and may lead to more serious problems later on.

○ Treat your children with empathy and compassion as they adjust, but do not over-indulge or fail to discipline them because of the divorce.

○ Avoid telling your child, "You're my little woman(or man), now that Mom (or Dad) and I have separated." Kids are kids and shouldn't be encouraged to act as if they are little grown-ups.

○ Encourage your child to participate in activities, sports and clubs. Help your child develop talents, social skills, and interests. Your child's natural development need not get derailed because of your divorce.

○ Develop your child's self-esteem by reinforcing good behavior and praising real accomplishments.

○ Being generous with false praise will never replace the sense of self-worth that comes from true achievement.

✪ Expect to hear repetitive questions from your children. Try not to lose patience if you find yourself giving the same answer over and over again.

✪ Repeated questions may indicate your children's efforts to overcome some alarming thoughts by having you remind them of what's really true. All children need reassurance during this difficult time.

✪ Although a full divorce recovery may take anywhere from 6 months to 2 years, if parents are attentive and empathic, most of the strong, initial reactions will abate within 4 to 6 weeks without the need for professional evaluation or therapy.

✪ If the initial problems persist for more than 4 to 6 weeks or seem to differ in kind or intensity from usual developmental problems, an evaluation by a therapist experienced in working with children is recommended.

Newborn to Age 3

✪ Infants cannot comprehend the concept of separation (thus, their reactions may be delayed) but if they are old enough to know who you are, they will be able to notice that Daddy or Mommy is not at home.

⚙ Even tiny infants can sense your emotional state, so make every effort to keep your disposition even.

⚙ Continuity is vitally important to infants and toddlers. Whichever parent had primary responsibility for the care of the young children before the separation should continue in this role.

⚙ Rather than jockeying for position as the custodian of their young children, parents should put aside their adult differences and co-operate to minimize the amount of disruption their infants and toddlers will experience.

⚙ Because absences can be terrifying to the very young, both parents need to maintain regular contact. Going more than one day without paying at least a short visit can be too much of an absence.

⚙ Needless to say, any caretaking changes which affect children in this age group should be made slowly and carefully.

⚙ If it is decided that travel between the homes is appropriate (*e.g.*, the child is now ready or old enough), each home should be furnished with a full set of the "necessities" - favorite rattles and toys, blankets, bedding, etc.

⚙ The same diet, feeding, nap and sleep schedule should be maintained from home to home.

⚙ Keep reassuring your children that Mommy and Daddy love them and will see them soon. Use a phrase that the child can "take" to the other home. For instance, blow a kiss as you say, "Take Mommy/Daddy 's kisses with you."

⚙ Do your best to allay fears that the parent who is away is "gone" or "lost" by arranging daily phone contact, making frequent visits, and explaining the concepts of "leaving" and "coming back" in age appropriate ways.

⚙ Be on the look-out for changes in your child's behavior that seem unusual or atypical given his/her developmental history.

⚙ Warning signs (loss of appetite, excessive crying, withdrawal, sleep disturbances) might mean you need to assess your co-parenting relationship (is the child picking up on your tension?) or revise the parenting schedule so that the child spends more time with the "missed" parent.

Ages 3 to 5

⚙ Although more independent, pre-school children still have a limited grasp of time and continue to be subject to abandonment fears.

⊙ Use "props" to communicate the concepts of continuity and stability, for instance, calendars showing "Mom's/Dad's days", so that your little ones can "see" the day when they will be at Dad's (or Mom's) again. Use toys, puppets, and figurines to demonstrate the concepts of leaving and returning.

⊙ Draw pictures together of families (or play with figurines); ask questions as you draw or play. As feelings come up, allow your child the space to say whatever comes to mind. Don't feel you have to make the "bad" feelings go away. Just listen and let your child know that he/she is understood. In many cases, just saying, "I can see why you feel like that," is helpful.

⊙ Don't argue with a child's feelings ("That's silly" or "No, no, no, don't feel that way"). Instead, be compassionate and understanding. Provide reassurance ("That must feel bad") and encourage discussion ("Maybe you should tell Mommy/Daddy how you feel about that").

⊙ Because they have difficulty recognizing and managing their feelings, children aged 3 to 5 sometimes exhibit regressive behavior or become aggressive.

○ Help your child identify and label internal states by looking at pictures of people who are calm, angry, happy, unhappy, relaxed, worried, secure or scared. Ask questions and take turns making up stories about the pictures.

○ If your children seem to be troubled, ask them about it. If you don't get an answer but suspect they're missing or angry at the other parent, gently suggest this and encourage action ("Maybe you're missing/angry at Daddy and could talk to him about this").

○ Find books at the local bookstore that are written for children on the subjects of divorce and expressing feelings. Among other things, these books will help you teach your children to express anger in ways that are constructive and appropriate (*e.g.*, outdoor physical activity, talking to the appropriate adult).

○ You will also learn not to rush in and "fix" your child's emotional states, but rather listen, empathize or reassure, and then let things be.

○ Even five miles between two homes can seem an enormous distance to a small child. Play games that illustrate the process of coming and going.

○ Have one chair at one end of the room be Daddy's home and one chair at the other end of the room be Mommy's home; play "going to Mommy's and going to Daddy's" by taking things back and forth between the two chairs, saying "hello" and "good-bye," sleeping over, etc.

○ Increase the space between the two chairs so that you are playing from room to room and Mommy's "home" can no longer be seen from Daddy's "home."

○ Be sure your children get the message that Mommy and Daddy always come back to pick them up and that nobody is going to be lost or go away.

○ Watch for signals that your child is having difficulty adjusting: regressive behavior, sleep problems, temper tantrums, excessive whining, clinging, changes in appetite, aggression.

○ Most children will demonstrate some problem behavior as they adjust to the divorce. Help them get their feelings out in the open, without insisting on a quick fix.

○ Problems that persist for more than 4 to 6 weeks, or which differ in kind or intensity from usual developmental concerns, may result from co-parenting tensions which have spilled over into your children's lives.

○ If you're certain that this is not the case, perhaps a revision of the parenting plan is in order. How is your child handling all the back and forth? Maybe he/she is not spending enough time with one of you. If the problem behavior continues, take your child for play therapy to help him/her work through this adjustment period.

Ages 5 to 8

○ Kindergartners and children in primary school can become overwhelmed with feelings of sadness and loss.

○ They are less likely to have an angry reaction at this age, although temper tantrums and defiance can surface as well.

○ Explanations need to be supplied and feelings need to be addressed. Since this age group understands more than their younger siblings, more questions will be asked and more details must be provided.

✪ The techniques described at pages 78 to 81 are also applicable to this age group. Please read these pages for advice on talking to your children and resolving adjustment issues.

✪ If your child is responding poorly, assess your co-parenting relationship. Are things between you and your co-parent strained or co-operative? Is the parenting plan working well?

✪ Check for deterioration of school relationships and school work. Alert your child's teacher and principal to your divorce and the changes in your family set-up.

✪ Even if your child seems to be managing well, watch for sleep problems, nightmares, stomach and headache complaints. Your child may be dealing with emotional problems in a physical way.

✪ Give your child a lot of empathy, reassurance, and attention. Be a good listener rather than a fixer.

✪ Be sure to spend enough quality time, including at least 30 minutes daily where you interact with your child at his/her eye level.

Ages 9 to 12

✪ The pre-adolescent wants more privacy, independence and autonomy than his/her younger siblings while remaining intensely loyal to each parent.

✪ These children may be both unhappy and angry about the divorce and begin to defy you.

✪ Children this age need clear limits and boundaries. When possible, work with your co-parent in setting and enforcing similar household rules. Beware, however, of running too tight a ship for fear of fomenting rebellion yourselves!

✪ Just as important as parents setting boundaries, is the need to instill in the children a sense of self-responsibility (setting up a chore system, for instance).

✪ Watch for non-participation in family activities, chores, school work, lying or stealing (often, a desperate cry for attention and help).

✪ Even though they can seem adult and as if they have everything under control, pre-adolescent children may be having a difficult time. Don't be fooled by appearances of maturity. Give pre-adolescents your time and compassion.

○ Try to engage your pre-adolescent in brief conversations about the divorce so as to avoid sup-
pression of feelings.

○ If you discuss some of your thoughts about the
divorce candidly (and age-appropriately), it's
likely that you'll hear some candid thoughts
from your child.

○ If your child is not responsive, try again later
(without being a pest and without making
mountains out of molehills). Remember, not
every emotion or behavioral problem is due to
your divorce!

Ages 13 to 18

○ One of the most important tasks of adolescence
is the child's separation and ultimate independence from his or her parents.

○ If this developmental process gets derailed, a
teenager may regress and fail to separate, or
may individuate prematurely and begin acting
out in pseudo-adult ways (replacing age-appropriate goals with drug use, inappropriate sexual
activity, truancy, or other rebellious activities).

○ Although teenagers may look adult, they are
not. Teenagers suffer from divorce-related problems just as their younger siblings do!

○ Continue to encourage openness and communication so that your teenagers do not repress their feelings, but speak with your teens about the divorce in an age appropriate way. Do not turn your older children into "pseudo-adults" or treat them as friends.

○ Because teens are coming to terms with their developing sexuality, they may be uncomfortable around a parent who is dating or embarking on an intimate relationship.

○ Whatever they may say to the contrary, your children want you to be their Mom or their Dad. Do not discuss your dates with them or otherwise attempt to amuse or interest them by sharing information about your personal life. Discretion is in order; don't treat your children as you would your friends, buddies, and confidantes.

○ Teenagers are more aware of parental reactions than their younger siblings and may be more affected by your moods and emotional difficulties than you realize.

○ Make every effort (within reason) to keep your disposition even around your children; share your more vulnerable side with other adults.

○ Continue to shield your teenagers from constant or intense parental discord. Ongoing parental fighting often leads to problem behavior, unconsciously designed to alert co-parents to the fact that they are more focused on their fighting and bickering than they are on their children's well-being.

○ If a teenager seems hopeless, irritable, apathetic, self-attacking, withdrawn, sleeping more/less than usual, eating more/less than usual, or easily moved to tears AND you sense that the symptoms go beyond what might ordinarily be expected from adolescents, consider that your child may be exhibiting signs of depression. If the symptoms persist, psychotherapy is advisable.

○ It is important that clear, firm, and reasonable limits be set for teenagers. Rebellious behavior can be a plea for firmer limits and more discipline.

○ Without compromising your particular parenting style, see if you and your co-parent can establish some similar house rules.

○ Do not encourage your teenager to believe that by going to the other parent's house, he/she can avoid responsibilities, chores, or penalties.

○ As children reach their teens, they are sometimes less willing to travel back and forth
between two homes. Teens may find the commuting increasingly difficult as a result of
social commitments, busier extra-curricular
schedules, expectations of friends, considera-
tions about clothing, books, etc.

○ If your teenager mentions that he/she does not
wish to go to your co-parent's because of a particular social commitment, have him/her take it
up directly with your co-parent.

○ If there are continuing problems with travel
back and forth between the two homes, the parenting plan may need to be re-evaluated.

○ In re-evaluating the plan, consider which of the
two parents is more available to be a caregiver
(who has a more flexible work schedule and
more time for supervision, who lives closer to
school). Do not simply rely on old formulas, for
instance, boys go with Dad, girls go with Mom.

○ Get your children's input and views, but
remember, you, not they, make the final decision. Even though your teenagers may have
strong opinions, they still need you to make
the rules and set the limits.

Personal Notes:

Personal Notes:

Chapter Ten

Managing
Your Feelings

⚙ It matters little that you anticipated the divorce or even that you initiated it, divorce is a traumatic event which will dramatically change your life.

⚙ Divorce churns up a parade of emotions including relief, confusion, jealousy, fear, grief, anger, envy, embarrassment, excitement, shame, regret, sadness, and guilt. Expect to take a long ride on an emotional roller coaster as you shift back and forth between powerful emotional states - feelings connected with divorce do not disappear overnight.

⚙ Many co-parents find the first two years after the break-up to be the most debilitating. Your relationship with your co-parent may dip to a new low as you wonder where your patience and parenting skills have gone. You may even begin to question your capacity to function as a rational, thinking adult.

○ Despite the fragility of your emotional state, the need for clear-headedness and resolve continues. You must run a household, deal with the reactions of family and friends, manage finances, raise your children, select an attorney, work out a parenting plan, negotiate support, divide property, consult with school officials, and so on.

○ During this time, your fledgling two home family might benefit from both parents meeting together with a professional counselor who has experience in the area of divorce.

○ There is a body of knowledge which now exists about divorce recovery. It can be very reassuring to know that the feelings you are experiencing are not unusual and that you are at a "normal" point in the recovery process.

○ Things will get better. Acceptance of your new family configuration and a smoothing out of the painful transitional phase usually occurs between 2 and 5 years after the separation.

○ By the end of the initial 2 to 5 years, you may have developed new competencies and skills, either in the workplace or at home, found more suitable employment, and worked through a good bit of your anger, fear, guilt, and/or sadness.

✪ At the point that you are able to look your co-parent in the eye and see a whole person with both good and bad qualities (rather than the devil incarnate or some other two-dimensional caricature of a person), you'll know you're well on the way to recovery.

Anger

✪ The reaction to the disappointment of a failed marriage often includes anger.

✪ Promises of intimate emotional, spiritual and physical communication as well as companionship and living "as a family" with your "ex" will now go unfulfilled.

✪ There are, of course, other divorce-related reasons for anger. Make an effort to understand what fuels your anger. Sometimes, simply identifying the reasons behind your anger can provide some relief.

✪ Are you angry because he/she didn't talk to you during the marriage?

✪ Are you angry because he/she didn't listen to you during the marriage?

✪ Are you angry because you feel betrayed or used?

○ Are you angry because everything didn't go your way in Court?

○ Are you angry because when you're not, you feel sad or frightened?

○ Are you angry for still other reasons? (you may find that some of your angry reactions have a history that predate your divorce).

○ Determine whether your anger is reasonable. Does your anger seem appropriate when you set forth the bare facts without the emotional overlay?

○ If your anger seems appropriate, ask yourself whether it would make sense to express it or whether there is little to be gained? If there is little to be gained (*e.g.*, yelling at a your "ex" for being late), count to 10, take a few deep breaths, and let it go.

○ It's vitally important to find a constructive way to express your anger. Repressing your anger may lead to health problems or cause you to become bitter, cynical, or depressed.

○ Repressed anger may also end up being misdirected at your children or other innocent parties.

❁ Unrestrained expressions of anger, on the other hand, are known to have negative effects on the cardiovascular system.

❁ When you have reason to be angry and have determined that it would make sense to express yourself, wait until the anger has subsided before taking action.

❁ In the meantime, think about how you might present the problem, including why it angers you, and some possible solutions.

❁ Communicate in a way that will enable you to be heard and understood (see Chapter 12, "Communication that Works").

❁ If you find yourself on "stress overload" and lashing out at the slightest provocation, remember to use relaxation techniques that have worked for you in the past (or check the self-help section of your bookstore or library for new ones).

❁ After a particularly difficult exchange with your co-parent, allow time for 5 minutes of deep breathing (inhale through your nose, hold for a count of 10, exhale slowly, repeat). Try this technique the next time you need to calm down.

○ While a certain level of anger is expectable and understandable as a means of relieving pressure and coping with emotional upset, pay close attention if - months after the divorce - you find yourself badmouthing or arguing with your "ex" at every opportunity.

○ Blaming your "ex" for all (or even nearly all) the problems which led to the divorce is unreasonable and unrealistic.

○ Accepting responsibility for your contribution to past problems will help you get through your anger, learn from your mistakes, and get on with your life.

○ Continuing hostility towards your "ex" may be your way of holding on to the marriage instead of grieving and letting go.

○ A support group or individual counseling may be able to help you understand what underlies your hostility so that you can begin to move on.

○ Intense, unrelenting rage that fills every conscious moment or which endures for weeks is dangerous.

○ Before you do serious harm to yourself or others, consult a therapist to help you work through this debilitating emotional state.

Fear

✪ Regardless of who is the initiator, the structure of your world change dramatically after you separate.

✪ In a relatively short period of time, you may need to find more suitable employment; develop additional skills and competencies as a new head of household; handle a difficult "ex"; and adjust to a host of unknowns concerning your children's well-being.

✪ Don't be surprised if your anxiety level temporarily skyrockets.

✪ Don't be too hard on yourself for being worried or apprehensive. Anxiety is natural under the circumstances.

✪ Set realistic goals for yourself, call upon people in your support network, and tell yourself that chaotic beginnings often produce impressive results.

✪ Do not make the mistake of waiting until you "feel like" doing something about your problems. Most of us do not enjoy looking for a new job or overhauling our careers. It's simply something that must be done.

❂ It's always difficult to face the unknown. Set your priorities anyway, putting the first steps on a "Goal Sheet" and tackling them one step at a time, regardless of how you feel.

❂ Even though you may be feeling anxious or "less than yourself," don't underestimate your capacity for change.

❂ Think of aptitudes and talents you have that might be transferable to a new job or career.

❂ Don't overlook skills you developed while volunteering, and be willing to develop some new competencies.

❂ If jobs you're looking for all require computer literacy, become computer literate. Consider other types of retraining or going back to school.

❂ Choose wisely among training programs and don't begrudge yourself the extra expense, you're investing in your future.

❂ If you continue to be beset with worries, take an inventory of your biggest concerns, write down in detail what you are saying to yourself on each subject, then evaluate the statements for truth and accuracy on a scale of 1 to 10.

○ For instance, if you are worried about finances and notice that you are telling yourself that you'll soon end up begging on a street corner, evaluate the begging scenario on a scale of 1 to 10, 10 being absolutely true, 1 being utterly ridiculous.

○ When you examine your thinking carefully, you'll be surprised at how often you scare yourself with false information.

○ Monitor your internal dialogue or "self-talk." Catch yourself in the act of spreading gloom and doom and tell yourself to stop.

○ Wear a rubber band around your wrist that you can snap whenever you find yourself making up worst case scenarios.

○ Counteract disquieting thoughts that have been induced by your worrying.

○ Visualize plausible, positive outcomes to situations which concern you.

○ When you get in the habit of challenging your negative self-talk, you'll undoubtedly prove the wisdom of the familiar remark, "I've been through a lot of bad things in my life and most of them have never happened."

✪ If you find yourself not sleeping for nights on end, unable to concentrate, and continually plagued by paralyzing worries, seek out the help of a support group.

✪ You will see and hear other survivors of divorce making it through similar crises and will benefit from the collective wisdom, support and guidance of the group.

✪ If a group setting is not for you, continue to rely on your support network or arrange some sessions of individual therapy to pull you through.

✪ Millions of others have been here and have survived. You will too; be patient and compassionate with yourself.

Guilt

✪ Co-parents who are mired in guilt may have difficulty setting appropriate limits and disciplining their children.

✪ As a guilt-ridden co-parent, you may find yourself flooded with pictures of your children's pained faces the day you walked out the door. You may overspend and assent to every request, just to assuage this discomfort.

⚙ Parenting fueled by guilt is harmful. Failure to provide secure and firm limits unwittingly fosters confusion, insecurity and a desire for experimentation (*e.g.*, "How far can I go?" "What can I get away with?"). This can have serious negative consequences for your child later on in life.

⚙ Ask yourself what underlies your guilt. If it's your role in ending the marriage, even though you were the parent to call it quits, you are continuing to play a major role in your children's two home family as an active and devoted co-parent.

⚙ You have not abandoned your children, and your relationship with them may actually improve as a result of the reconfiguration of your original household.

⚙ If you are blaming yourself for causing the break-up, beware of taking on more than your share of the responsibility.

⚙ No relationship ends because 1 person was 100% at fault; more often than not, responsibility is more evenly divided.

⚙ Consider the ways in which your co-parent had a less obvious, more subtle role in bringing about the end of the marriage.

○ While a certain amount of remorse is inevitable, appropriate, and useful, guilt that continues without end is irrational and usually has other, deeper causes.

○ This is something you must come to terms with, either by your own self-understanding or through the help of a wise friend or professional counselor.

Sadness

○ The divorce experience can feel similar to the experience of other major losses, such as the death of someone you love.

○ The process of mourning may include shock and disbelief; tears, lethargy and depression; anxiety and panic; social withdrawal; and anger. Do not attempt to escape the normal grieving process by workaholism, excessive or inappropriate socializing, incessant fighting, over-involvement with your children, or other forms of denial.

○ Give yourself time to think about your marriage and divorce - your hopes, dreams, losses and disappointments as well as all the changes you are adjusting to. Allow yourself to fully experience the feelings that come up for you. A good cry is not only cleansing but essential if you are to release, rather than suppress, your sadness.

⊙ Do not be afraid of intense feeling states; no feeling lasts forever, and nobody ever died from a feeling.

⊙ Pay attention to your inner voice and write down what you're telling yourself. Carefully evaluate the negative statements.

⊙ Identify exaggerations and over-generalizations rather than accepting this "self-talk" as truth. Your life is not over.

⊙ Continue to explore your feelings in a journal or by talking with caring friends.

⊙ Tell yourself your divorce was for the best. Your kids will not be observing a "dead" marriage and will have more quality time with both of you.

⊙ As co-parents, you will both appreciate your children more.

⊙ Reformat negative images and turn them into positives, *e.g.*, instead of seeing yourself as alone, you might appreciate that you have a certain freedom as a result of your divorce.

⊙ Take advantage of the fact that you can do things now that you were unable to do as a full-time parent.

✪ Plan appropriately for the times your children will not be at your house.

✪ Call on people in your support network who will be there for you whether you need help or just a sounding board.

✪ Whatever you do, don't isolate yourself. People tend to magnify their problems when left to their own devices.

✪ If you've neglected your physical health and well-being, go for a check-up and attend to whatever needs attending.

✪ Make time for yourself! Pursue longstanding interests and activities that you abandoned due to your spouse's lack of enthusiasm or interest. Join a health club, go out dancing, play basketball, take up tennis, start walking, go camping, eat to protect your health and heart.

✪ If you find yourself unable to move on or are otherwise "stuck" in your sadness, fear, loneliness, numbness, or lethargy, look for a support group or therapist to help you get past the most difficult hurdles. Don't lose hope, you'll get through this!

✪ Remember, the more you try to avoid, deny or escape your "difficult" emotional states, the longer they will persist and the longer your divorce recovery will take.

Personal Notes:

Personal Notes:

Chapter Eleven

The "Problem" Co-Parent

☙ Because you will always have a relationship with your "ex," it is critical that you find a way to manage your interactions so that they are more productive and less upsetting.

☙ Think of your "ex" as your co-parenting partner. The two of you have a job to do. When problems and disagreements develop, do your best to deal with them in a thoughtful, business-like manner. Let your most sophisticated problem-solving skills and powers of persuasion, not your emotions, get you where you need to go.

☙ Tell yourself that any difficulty you're having with your co-parent is not a catastrophe but is rather a "problem" (you can solve a problem, not a catastrophe).

✪ Make the distinction between problems and catastrophes and then set about solving your problems, reminding yourself that solutions may take time.

✪ Ask yourself, "Is there any other way of looking at this situation?"

✪ Consider your own behavior. In what ways are you a "problem co-parent"? Is your tone hostile or sarcastic? Your presentation self-righteous, accusatory, or rude? Your demeanor condescending or impatient?

✪ Are you still blaming your "ex"? If so, take responsibility for your own emotions; you cannot go through life blaming your "ex" for a set of feelings you are having.

✪ Bear in mind the personality style of the person with whom you're dealing. There's no reason to suppose that your co-parent's way of relating to you will change dramatically after your divorce.

✪ If your co-parent was somebody who criticized rather than supported you in times of crisis, expect repeat performances.

✪ If he/she constantly interrupted you or barely communicated during the marriage, expect more of the same.

✿ If he/she scarcely paid attention to you, expect this to continue. If he/she was never punctual, don't expect punctuality.

✿ In fact, you can count on things being a bit worse during the first 1 to 2 years after separation.

✿ Accept your co-parent as he/she is. Keep all of his/her shortcomings and limitations clearly in mind.

✿ This way you won't be blindsided by the faults and problem behaviors, and you won't mistakenly assume that your co-parent has changed in some way since you separated.

✿ Don't participate when your co-parent attempts to engage you in heated exchanges or screaming matches. Instead, take a mental step backwards and try to understand what motivates the problem behavior before responding (See Chapter 10, "Working through Your Feelings : Anger").

✿ If your co-parent is the type who is constantly giving you stage directions about the "right" way to parent the children, remind yourself that anxiety underlies his/her need for control and attempt to allay the anxiety.

○ For example, your co-parent is attempting to control the children's TV watching in your house. Instead of fighting back, you might say "I think you are worried about the kids doing well in school. Please don't worry. I am doing everything I can so that they do well. I'm 100% with you on this."

○ If your co-parent is sarcastic, sullen, withholding, or defensive, instead of attacking or responding in kind, remind yourself that she/he is still having a difficult time adjusting to the divorce. This will help you to let things go and get on with the business at hand.

○ You needn't listen to anyone who is yelling or verbally abusive. Warn your co-parent that you will not participate in any conversations that involve yelling or profanity since these exchanges are unproductive and only foster ill-will. Make it clear that you will resume the discussion only when things have quieted down.

○ Set limits. Leave the scene, put down the phone, temporarily turn off the ringer, and disconnect your answering machine.

○ If you feel physically threatened, change your locks, get a restraining order, call a friend or neighbor (or the police, if the situation warrants, and immediately remove yourself and your children to a place of safety).

✪ If you repeatedly find yourself in explosive situations with your co-parent (or others), consider group or individual psychotherapy to get to the bottom of what precipitates these dangerous encounters and how best to avoid them.

✪ Give up your efforts to banish a problem co-parent (who is also a devoted parent) from your life or your children's life. As time goes by and your co-parenting relationship improves, you'll be grateful for your co-parent's devotion to the children and wonder why you ever wished for his/her disappearance in the first place.

✪ The under-involved co-parent presents a different problem. Children will be disappointed, angered, and potentially harmed by a parent's chronic lateness, lack of interest, or failure to maintain adequate contact.

✪ If you suspect that your co-parent's lack of involvement is related to an incomplete or unsatisfactory adjustment to the divorce, explain this to your children in an age-appropriate way. ("It can take time for grown-ups to adjust to divorce too. My hope is that Dad/Mom will be around more after several months have passed and things have settled down a bit").

✪ In the interim, do what you can to rekindle your co-parent's interest, devotion, and commitment to the children. Your goal is to keep the connection as "alive" as you can.

○ With this in mind, send report cards, photos, tapes, completed homework and school projects. Call or send reminders about school events, birthdays, Little League games, gymnastics recitals, and other important events in your child's life.

○ Remind your co-parent that children who grow up with an absent, uncaring, or under-involved parent often develop depression and other psychological problems later in life.

○ Encourage your children to maintain contact by telephone calls, letters and birthday cards, and when appropriate, by communicating their upset directly to your co-parent.

○ Be persistent, but avoid judging and criticizing. Your goal is not to start a fight but rather to focus your co-parent's attention on the importance of his/her presence in your child's life. Confrontations and attacks are unlikely to accomplish this.

○ If your co-parent's behavior shows no sign of improvement, do not attempt to alleviate your child's pain or anger by making excuses ("Mom/Dad loves you so much, it's just that...").

○ Instead, give truthful, age-appropriate explanations. Children may be young and inexperienced but they understand what love and devotion feel like. They know that Moms and Dads who love their children make time for them.

○ Making constant excuses for your co-parent's behavior teaches your children to deny their feelings and question their perceptions.

○ Let your children know that adults who fail to maintain adequate contact with their children have problems and are to be pitied rather than censured. This will help your children stop blaming themselves for "causing" the under-involvement (*e.g.*, "If I had been a better child, Mom/Dad would want to spend time with me").

○ To further offset feelings of rejection and low self-esteem that can arise, strive to maintain relationships with other caring, mature adults who will model devotion and reliability to your children.

Personal Notes:

Personal Notes:

Chapter Twelve

Communication that Works

⊕ Effective communication is the cornerstone of any good relationship; a good co-parenting relationship is no exception.

⊕ If your relationship with your co-parent is strained or hostile, strive to present yourself in a mature and business-like manner, reminding yourself that calmness pays off in the long run.

⊕ For example, although your co-parent is being abrupt with you, you might decide that he or she is still listening. If you continue making your points without "taking the bait," you might find that your calmness and resolve pay off.

⊕ You do not have to be buddies to communicate effectively. You do, however, have to stop arguing, bickering, sniping, and criticizing if you entertain any hope of improving the quality of your relationship.

✪ Try to forget that you had a history as husband and wife and think of yourselves as joint-caregivers who must cooperate for the benefit of your children.

✪ Communicate frequently with your co-parent so that he/she is aware of what you and the children have been doing.

✪ Let your co-parent know how school, homework, and friendships are coming along and what issues and feelings are surfacing with the kids.

✪ If both parents know what's going on in both homes, the children will have a less fractured experience of their new family life and parents will be better equipped to be caretakers.

✪ Because each parent will have a general sense of what is transpiring in each household, children will be less able to manipulate or play one parent off against the other.

✪ In the early stages of co-parenting, you may find even neutral conversations with your co-parent to be difficult or unpleasant.

⊙ If so, fax or send a "news update" to your co-parent. In your update, describe what transpired during your time together— pleasurable activities as well as any problems, questions, or appointments which should be communicated in the interests of good co-parenting.

⊙ If you have a disagreement with your co-parent or a difficult issue to discuss, wait for an opportune time, you're more likely to find a receptive ear. Set out the facts, talk about yourself and your feelings only ("I" statements), then make your request.

⊙ The phrase "I" statements describes statements that refer primarily to the feelings and beliefs of the speaker, as opposed to those which blame, attack, or otherwise disparage the listener. Because of their self-referential quality, "I" statements foster discussion rather than defensiveness or counter-attack.

⊙ For example, "I'm upset about your non-attendance at Joey's school conferences. Can you make it a point to be at the next one?" is an "I" statement followed by a request. On the other hand, "It's ridiculous the way you're always missing things at Joey's school. You're so selfish!" is an attack and will only arouse the listener's ill-will.

○ Criticisms thinly disguised as "I" statements will also have negative effects. For instance, "I feel that you've been totally irresponsible," is a wolf in sheep's clothing. This is not an "I" statement but rather an accusation!

○ Ask sincere, open-ended questions and wait to hear your co-parent's response.

○ Paraphrase your co-parent's response before making your own. Even though listening and paraphrasing are not the equivalent of agreeing, they give your co-parent the feeling that you are a respectful and thoughtful audience.

○ For example, Co-parent A says, "Lately all Danny talks about is baseball. He says you've told him to practice all the time and he seems nervous at games and practices. Maybe he should stop for a while." Co-parent B responds, "What I think you're saying is that I'm putting too much pressure on Danny in Little League. Okay, I hear that. Let me respond this way...."

○ Give each other roughly equal time to make points. Agree in advance not to interrupt, no matter how tempting; each of you will have a chance to speak. Listen, rather than closing your ears, hardening your heart, and planning your rebuttal!

❂ Don't muddy the waters by bringing up several problems at once.

❂ If one of you is getting angry, say so, and suggest resuming the discussion another day. Politely end the discussion (or calmly put down the phone) if the conversation becomes hostile and unproductive.

❂ Think of defusers and solutions, not zingers and insults. It's no credit to you that you "let him have it" or that you really "got her" during your last exchange. What do you accomplish by having yet another fight?

❂ If a particular discussion has escalated into an argument (not unusual in the early stages of co-parenting), continue the discussion in writing, following the rules enumerated earlier (be courteous, businesslike, and stick to the issues at hand).

❂ Before you send off your written communication, have a friend evaluate it. You may be more aggressive (or conciliatory) than you realize. Particularly serious or sensitive topics may need a lawyer's attention.

❂ The same conditions that apply to communications with your co-parent apply to communications with your children.

⊕ That is, bring up touchy subjects at times when they are likely to be heard. Use "I" statements instead of making accusations or criticizing. Listen without interrupting and stay with one issue at a time.

⊕ Starting conversations when either parent or child is upset, tired, busy, or distracted is likely to result in misunderstandings and unpleasantness.

⊕ Look for workable solutions to the problems you are having. Be willing to consider compromise when compromise is appropriate (a real compromise means you have to give up something too!). If you're stuck, consult a trusted friend, therapist, or mediator. The objectivity you get from a neutral third party can make a world of difference.

⊕ Accept the fact that your co-parent has some measure of power over you (for instance, he/she can continue to "bait" you by doing all the things that irritate you and make life difficult).

⊕ Realize there is little you can do to "make" your co-parent behave in a more constructive or mature manner. Just keep telling yourself that you are working towards the day when he/she no longer has the need to misbehave. It will come!

✪ In the meantime, take a look at your own behavior. What might you be doing to fan the flames? Does your attitude need work?"

✪ Maybe you need to drop the tough, "never say die" stance.

✪ Maybe you need to be tougher and set clearer limits.

✪ Maybe you need to lighten up and stop making mountains out of molehills.

✪ Maybe you need to stop taking the "bait."

✪ Maybe you need to ask for help in tackling some very serious issues (friends, family, a therapist, an attorney).

✪ Maybe you need to give up being "right" in the interests of having a co-parenting relationship that works.

Personal Notes:

Personal Notes:

Order Form

fax   Fax orders: (818) 909-9209. Please use this form.

✉   Postal orders: WinnSpeed Press
                14622 Ventura Blvd., Ste. 329
                Sherman Oaks, CA 91403.
                Please use this form.

Please send the following: ***Co-Parenting after Divorce***

To (your name): _____

Company name: _____

Address: _____

City: _____ **State:** _____ **Zip:** _____ - _____

Telephone: (_____) _____

Price per copy: $12.95.
Orders of 10 or more: $9.95 per copy.

Quantity: _____ books

Sales tax: Please add 7.75% for books shipped to CA addresses.

Shipping: Book Rate: $2.00 for the first book, $.75 each
             additional book. (surface shipping may take 3-4
             weeks). Air mail: $3.50 per book

                           Subtotal: _____

                         Sales Tax: _____

                          Shipping: _____

                              Total: _____

Please allow 4-6 weeks for your order to be processed.

Payment:

Cheque #: _____

Credit card: (please indicate with a check mark)
        □ Visa   □ MasterCard   □ Discover

Card number: _____

Name on card: _____

Expiration date: _____